Addresses

Addresses

AMISH

THE ART OF THE QUILT

Maxwell Macmillan Canada
Toronto

Macmillan Publishing Company
New York

in association with
Callaway, New York

Maxwell Macmillan International
New York Oxford Singapore Sydney

Introduction and captions by Julie Silber
Edited by Caissa Douwes and Natacha Vassilchikov
Art direction and design by Tamotsu Yagi

———————————

Julie Silber is a lecturer, author and curator with twenty-five years' experience collecting and studying quilts. She is the curator of the Esprit Quilt Collection in San Francisco and the associate producer of the film *Hearts and Hands*. She was a curator of "AMISH: The Art of the Quilt" at The Fine Arts Museums of San Francisco in 1990.

———————————

Photograph and text arrangement copyright © 1991 by Julie Silber. All rights reserved. No part of this book may be reproduced or transmitted in any form or by any means electronic or mechanical, including photocopying, recording, or by any information storage and retrieval system, without permission in writing from the Publisher. Photographs and text copyright © 1990 by Esprit De Corp. used by permission.
Published in the United States by Macmillan Publishing Company, 866 Third Avenue, New York, NY 10022, in association with Callaway Editions, Inc., 54 Seventh Avenue South, New York, NY 10014, and simultaneously in Canada by Maxwell Macmillan Canada, Inc., 1200 Eglinton Avenue East, Suite 200, Don Mills, Ontario M3C 3N1.
Macmillan Publishing Company is part of the Maxwell Communication Group of Companies.
ISBN 0-02-079862-8
Produced under the direction of Nicholas Callaway and True Sims. Production coordination by Caissa Douwes and Natacha Vassilchikov, with assistance from Barbara Bergeron.
Art direction, typographic design and layout by Tamotsu Yagi, assisted by DelRae Roth.
Typesetting by Display Lettering + Copy, San Francisco.
Color photography by Sharon Risedorph and Lynn Kellner.
Printed in Japan by Nissha Printing Company, Ltd., Kyoto.
Front Cover: Lone Star, Unknown Amish quiltmaker, American, Lancaster County, Pennsylvania, Circa 1920, Pieced cottons, 88 x 89 inches, 585.001.
Frontispiece: Double Ninepatch, Unknown Amish quiltmaker, American, Lancaster County, Pennsylvania, Circa 1900, Pieced wools, 70 x 82 inches, 585.235.

PERSONAL INFORMATION

Name

Home Address

City   State   Zip

Telephone

Office Address

City   State   Zip

Telephone

Social Security Number

Emergency Numbers

NOTES

INTRODUCTION

Quilts are textiles composed of three layers of cloth held together by knots or stitches. In the eighteenth and nineteenth centuries, virtually all North American women—women of every age, class, region and ethnic origin—took up the needle to create works that were bedcoverings and more. All of these quilts have within their stitches a great deal to tell us about the lives and times of the women who made them and the people who lived with them.

Few quilts, however, are as easily recognized as those made by the Amish. A "plain" religious group who adhere to and live their principles of simplicity, practicality, humility and nonresistance, the Amish emigrated from Germany and Switzerland in the eighteenth and nineteenth centuries, settling in the rich farmlands of Pennsylvania and the Midwest. From about 1870 to 1960, the women of this rural culture, particularly those in Lancaster County, Pennsylvania, produced an extraordinary kind of quilt.

Amish women were restricted by tradition from using printed fabrics, and were also discouraged from engaging in the "worldly" practice of sewing together many small pieces in their quilts. Within these limitations, however, they created quilts of remarkable purity, vitality and power from abstract geometric arrangements of solid-color fabrics. Using the fine wools from which they also sewed their clothing, they drew from a palette that is rich and saturated, subtle and glowing.

Aesthetics is a part of Amish life; in Lancaster it is shaped by a commitment to excellence in workmanship and the highly held values of fellowship and community. Conformity, in quiltmaking and throughout Amish life, ensures harmony. There are very few absolutely unique Amish quilts. We find adaptations and combinations of only a few traditional patterns, rather than wholly new designs, in these quilts. In quiltmaking, as in all of Amish life, behavior that reinforces a sense of unity and fellowship is valued more highly than an individual's innovation or unique achievement.

Robert Hughes, the renowned art critic, says of Amish quilts, "In their complexity, visual intensity and quality of craftsmanship, such works simply dispel the notion that folk art is innocent social birdsong. They are as much a part of the story of high aesthetic effort in America as any painting or sculpture." We warmly invite you to enjoy in this address book one of America's purest and finest forms of artistic expression.

Julie Silber

SUGGESTED READING

Bishop, Robert, and Elizabeth Safanda, *A Gallery of Amish Quilts.* New York: E. P. Dutton, Inc., 1976.

Ferrero, Pat, Elaine Hedges, and Julie Silber, *Hearts and Hands.* San Francisco: The Quilt Digest Press, 1987.

Granick, Eve Wheatcroft, *The Amish Quilt.* Intercourse, Pennsylvania: Good Books, Inc., 1989.

Hostetler, John A., *Amish Society.* 3rd ed. Baltimore: Johns Hopkins University Press, 1980.

Kraybill, Donald B., *The Riddle of Amish Culture.* Baltimore: Johns Hopkins University Press, 1989.

McCauley, Daniel and Kathryn, *Decorative Arts of the Amish of Lancaster County.* Intercourse, Pennsylvania: Good Books, Inc., 1988.

Pellman, Rachel and Kenneth, *The World of Amish Quilts.* Intercourse, Pennsylvania: Good Books, Inc., 1984.

Pottinger, David, *Quilts from the Indiana Amish.* New York: E. P. Dutton, Inc., 1983.

Silber, Julie, *The Esprit Quilt Collection.* San Francisco: Esprit de Corp., 1985.

Silber, Julie, and Robert Hughes, *AMISH: The Art of the Quilt.* New York: Knopf/Callaway, 1990.

Swank, Scott, ed., *Arts of the Pennsylvania Germans.* New York: W. W. Norton and Co., 1983.

Diamond in the Square

Unknown Amish quiltmaker, American, Lancaster County, Pennsylvania, Circa 1920,
Pieced wools, 78 x 78 inches, 585.103

This is a very pure example of the simple Diamond, the essence perhaps. Here we see the intense, glowing colors for which twentieth-century Lancaster quilts are known. Some students of Lancaster society report that the Amish sometimes call the Diamond design "Cape," or in their dialect "Halstuch," a reference to the shape of the traditional shawl the women wear over their shoulders.

A

Name

Address

Telephone

Name

Address

Telephone

Name

Address

Telephone

Name

Address

Telephone

A

Name

Address

Telephone

Name

Address

Telephone

Name

Address

Telephone

Name

Address

Telephone

Name

Address

Telephone

Name

Address

Telephone

Name

Address

Telephone

Name

Address

Telephone

A

Name

Address

Telephone

Name

Address

Telephone

Name

Address

Telephone

Name

Address

Telephone

A

Name

Address

Telephone

Name

Address

Telephone

Name

Address

Telephone

Name

Address

Telephone

A

Name

Address

Telephone

Name

Address

Telephone

Name

Address

Telephone

Name

Address

Telephone

Diamond in the Square (Variation)

Unknown Amish quiltmaker, American, Lancaster County, Pennsylvania, Circa 1930,
Pieced wools and cottons, 79 x 79 inches, 585.072

We find adaptations and combinations of only a few traditional patterns, rather than wholly new designs, in Amish quilts. In quiltmaking, as in every aspect of Amish life, behavior that reinforces a sense of unity and fellowship is valued more highly than an individual's innovation or unique achievement. Here, in addition to the multicolored center, the quiltmaker used seven colors and added every possible traditional border and corner.

B

Name

Address

Telephone

Name

Address

Telephone

Name

Address

Telephone

Name

Address

Telephone

B

Name

Address

Telephone

Name

Address

Telephone

Name

Address

Telephone

Name

Address

Telephone

Name

Address

Telephone

Name

Address

Telephone

Name

Address

Telephone

Name

Address

Telephone

B

Name

Address

Telephone

Name

Address

Telephone

Name

Address

Telephone

Name

Address

Telephone

B a r s

Unknown Amish quiltmaker, American, Lancaster County, Pennsylvania, Circa 1930,
Pieced wools, 78 x 80 inches, 585.198

The basic Lancaster Amish Bars pattern has seven inner stripes. In this variation, known as Split Bars, every other stripe is divided into three sections. While this particular modification is seen less often than the simple Bars, it is not rare. The narrow inner frame here is also divided, echoing the Split Bars in the middle section and creating yet another variation on the basic Bars pattern.

C

Name

Address

Telephone

Name

Address

Telephone

Name

Address

Telephone

Name

Address

Telephone

C

Name

Address

Telephone

Name

Address

Telephone

Name

Address

Telephone

Name

Address

Telephone

Name

Address

Telephone

Name

Address

Telephone

Name

Address

Telephone

Name

Address

Telephone

C

Name

Address

Telephone

Name

Address

Telephone

Name

Address

Telephone

Name

Address

Telephone

Double Irish Chain

Unknown Amish quiltmaker, American, Lancaster County, Pennsylvania, Circa 1920,
Pieced wools, 70 x 83 inches, 585.215

The Double Irish Chain design is a simple Twentyfive Patch with a few squares appliquéd to the plain alternate block to complete the diagonal "chain." This has the deep, radiant tones and superb quilting that typify Lancaster quilts. It floats within a single wide border and is finished with a wide binding, which is characteristically of a contrasting color.

D

Name

Address

Telephone

Name

Address

Telephone

Name

Address

Telephone

Name

Address

Telephone

D

Name

Address

Telephone

Name

Address

Telephone

Name

Address

Telephone

Name

Address

Telephone

D

Name

Address

Telephone

Name

Address

Telephone

Name

Address

Telephone

Name

Address

Telephone

D

Name

Address

Telephone

Name

Address

Telephone

Name

Address

Telephone

Name

Address

Telephone

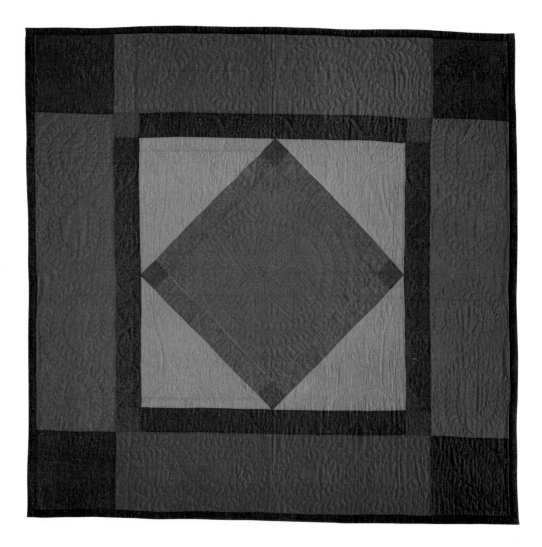

Diamond in the Square

*Unknown Amish quiltmaker, American, Lancaster County, Pennsylvania, Circa 1920–30,
Pieced wools, 77 x 77 inches, 585.167*

Lancaster County Amish women loved the elegantly simple Diamond in the Square pattern and made it again and again from the late nineteenth century through the 1960s. Because it was so popular with them and only they made it, Diamond is the pattern most closely associated with the Amish in Lancaster County. This one has a clear, almost sparkling feeling, which the quiltmaker achieved by her particular arrangement of color.

E

Name

Address

Telephone

Name

Address

Telephone

Name

Address

Telephone

Name

Address

Telephone

E

Name

Address

Telephone

Name

Address

Telephone

Name

Address

Telephone

Name

Address

Telephone

E

Name

Address

Telephone

Name

Address

Telephone

Name

Address

Telephone

Name

Address

Telephone

E

Name

Address

Telephone

Name

Address

Telephone

Name

Address

Telephone

Name

Address

Telephone

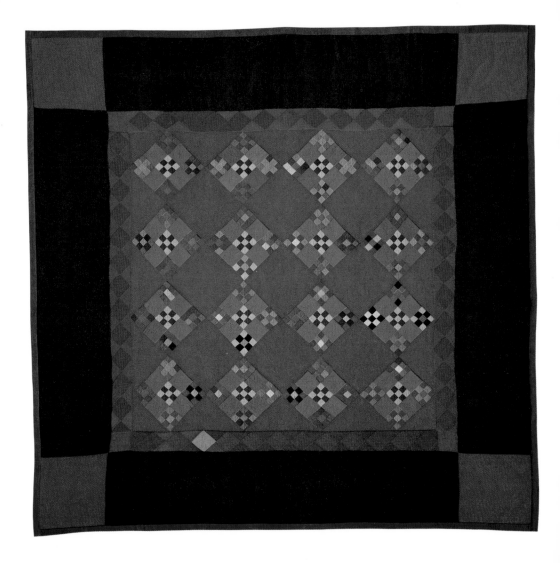

D o u b l e   N i n e p a t c h

Made by Dorothy Beiler, Amish quiltmaker, American, Lancaster County, Pennsylvania, Circa 1929,
Pieced wools and rayons, 80 x 82 inches, 585.005

When we got this quilt, we were given the maker's name but, unfortunately, nothing to help explain why Dorothy Beiler included one light blue diamond in the border. It is rare for a Lancaster Amish quilt to have an "outstanding" piece. Even in quilts using many different colors, Amish quiltmakers strove for overall balance and harmony rather than call attention to any one area.

F

Name

Address

Telephone

Name

Address

Telephone

Name

Address

Telephone

Name

Address

Telephone

F

Name

Address

Telephone

Name

Address

Telephone

Name

Address

Telephone

Name

Address

Telephone

Name

Address

Telephone

Name

Address

Telephone

Name

Address

Telephone

Name

Address

Telephone

F

Name

Address

Telephone

Name

Address

Telephone

Name

Address

Telephone

Name

Address

Telephone

B a r s

Unknown Amish quiltmaker, American, Lancaster County, Pennsylvania, Circa 1940,
Pieced wools, 79 x 87 inches, 585.035

Stitched flowers and vines climb the green stripe in this Split Bars, the quilting a delicate counterpoint to the hard, angular lines of the piecework. Amish women sometimes worked almost inconspicuous changes of color into their quilts, using slightly different shades, as with the reds here.

G

Name

Address

Telephone

Name

Address

Telephone

Name

Address

Telephone

Name

Address

Telephone

G

Name

Address

Telephone

Name

Address

Telephone

Name

Address

Telephone

Name

Address

Telephone

Name

Address

Telephone

Name

Address

Telephone

Name

Address

Telephone

Name

Address

Telephone

G

Name

Address

Telephone

Name

Address

Telephone

Name

Address

Telephone

Name

Address

Telephone

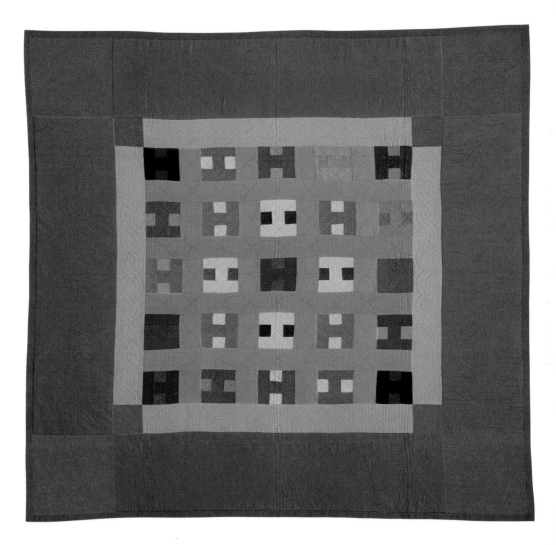

"H" Quilt

Unknown Amish quiltmaker, American, Lancaster County, Pennsylvania, Circa 1940–50,
Pieced cottons, 78 x 78 inches, 585.300

Except for this one, patterns based on letters of the alphabet are unknown among the Amish. But such patterns are part of the "English" (the term for people outside the Amish faith) quilt vocabulary, in which the letter represents sometimes a family initial, sometimes an organization or concept. In American quilts, the "T" design, for example, could signify an allegiance with the temperance movement.

Name

Address

Telephone

Name

Address

Telephone

Name

Address

Telephone

Name

Address

Telephone

H

Name

Address

Telephone

Name

Address

Telephone

Name

Address

Telephone

Name

Address

Telephone

H

Name

Address

Telephone

Name

Address

Telephone

Name

Address

Telephone

Name

Address

Telephone

H

Name

Address

Telephone

Name

Address

Telephone

Name

Address

Telephone

Name

Address

Telephone

Diamond in the Square

Unknown Amish quiltmaker, American, Lancaster County, Pennsylvania, Circa 1910–20,
Pieced wools, 81 x 81 inches, 585.275

The Amish are conservative in a cultural sense: they are uncomfortable with change. A traditional culture, they prefer the old to the new in both their religious and their social lives, so the Lancaster County Amish made only a few quilt patterns and variations on those patterns. Within very strict limitations of form, however, Amish quiltmakers made personal aesthetic decisions regarding colors, color placement, quilting and format. This piece was purchased in Intercourse, Pennsylvania, from an Amish woman who observed that the quilting in it is "exceptional, even for an Amish quilt."

Name

Address

Telephone

Name

Address

Telephone

Name

Address

Telephone

Name

Address

Telephone

I-J

Name

Address

Telephone

Name

Address

Telephone

Name

Address

Telephone

Name

Address

Telephone

Name

Address

Telephone

Name

Address

Telephone

Name

Address

Telephone

Name

Address

Telephone

I-J

Name

Address

Telephone

Name

Address

Telephone

Name

Address

Telephone

Name

Address

Telephone

Sunshine and Shadow

Unknown Amish quiltmaker, American, Lancaster County, Pennsylvania, Circa 1930–40,
Pieced wools, cottons and rayons, 79 x 79 inches, 585.003

Sunshine and Shadow, one of the four or five most commonly made designs in Lancaster, offers the quiltmaker exciting possibilities for manipulating color. This example has lots of contrast; compare it with the Sunshine and Shadow in the letter R to see how two quiltmakers' different personalities emerge. The center of this piece is slightly diffuse; many other Sunshine and Shadow quilts have a distinct piece, set apart by its color, at the very center.

K

Name

Address

Telephone

Name

Address

Telephone

Name

Address

Telephone

Name

Address

Telephone

K

Name

Address

Telephone

Name

Address

Telephone

Name

Address

Telephone

Name

Address

Telephone

Name

Address

Telephone

Name

Address

Telephone

Name

Address

Telephone

Name

Address

Telephone

K

Name

Address

Telephone

Name

Address

Telephone

Name

Address

Telephone

Name

Address

Telephone

B a r s

Unknown Amish quiltmaker, American, Lancaster County, Pennsylvania, Circa 1940,
Pieced wools, 75 x 75 inches, 585.057

Amish women in Lancaster County often included subtle color changes in their quilts, which you can miss if you are not looking closely. Here, the pink and lavender in the inner frame are very close in shade. Although many all-wool Lancaster quilts are early ones, the simplified, stylized floral quilting and the pastel colors of this Bars indicate that it is probably a later piece.

Name

Address

Telephone

Name

Address

Telephone

Name

Address

Telephone

Name

Address

Telephone

L

Name

Address

Telephone

Name

Address

Telephone

Name

Address

Telephone

Name

Address

Telephone

L

Name

Address

Telephone

Name

Address

Telephone

Name

Address

Telephone

Name

Address

Telephone

L

Name

Address

Telephone

Name

Address

Telephone

Name

Address

Telephone

Name

Address

Telephone

L o n e   S t a r

Unknown Amish quiltmaker, American, Lancaster County, Pennsylvania, Circa 1920,
Pieced wools, 88 x 89 inches, 585.001

The Lone Star, a pattern borrowed from the "English," appears infrequently in Lancaster County Amish
quilts. Its strong central motif is compatible with Lancaster sensibilities, but there is often a pulsating,
outward energy in the Lone Star that may contradict the usual quiet, interior feeling of their quilts.
The dynamic movement, achieved by the careful placement of color, is finally contained here by
the weight of the darker plum border.

M

Name

Address

Telephone

Name

Address

Telephone

Name

Address

Telephone

Name

Address

Telephone

M

Name

Address

Telephone

Name

Address

Telephone

Name

Address

Telephone

Name

Address

Telephone

Name

Address

Telephone

Name

Address

Telephone

Name

Address

Telephone

Name

Address

Telephone

M

Name

Address

Telephone

Name

Address

Telephone

Name

Address

Telephone

Name

Address

Telephone

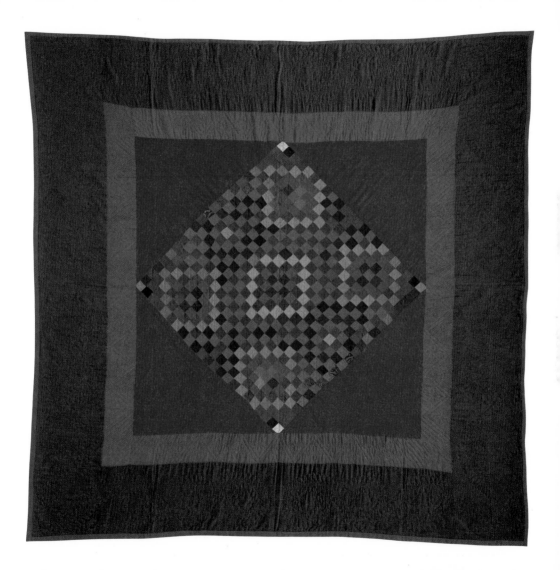

Diamond in the Square (Variation)

*Made by Fanny Petersheim, Amish quiltmaker, American, Lancaster County, Pennsylvania, Circa 1920,
Pieced wools and rayons, 90 x 90 inches, 585.110*

Fanny Petersheim (1879-1941) left us a most unusual quilt—a Diamond filled with a design called
Philadelphia Pavement, a series of little Sunshine and Shadows. The central design becomes a bit more
orderly when looked at from an angle, but it is still far more "askew" than most Lancaster quilts,
known for their symmetry and precision.

Name

Address

Telephone

Name

Address

Telephone

Name

Address

Telephone

Name

Address

Telephone

N

Name

Address

Telephone

Name

Address

Telephone

Name

Address

Telephone

Name

Address

Telephone

Name

Address

Telephone

Name

Address

Telephone

Name

Address

Telephone

Name

Address

Telephone

N

Name

Address

Telephone

Name

Address

Telephone

Name

Address

Telephone

Name

Address

Telephone

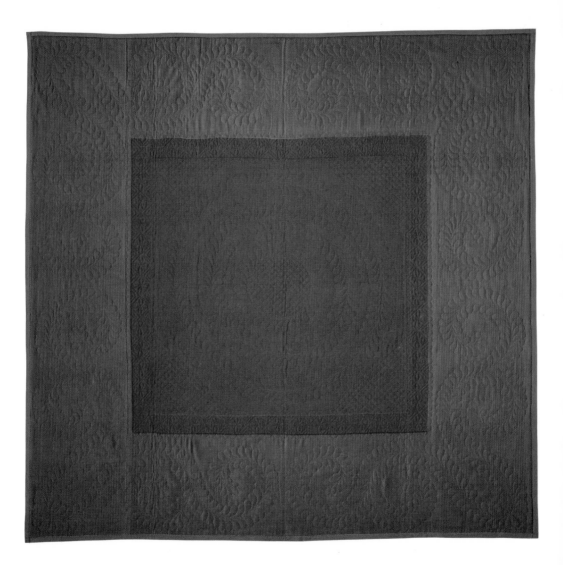

C e n t e r   S q u a r e

Unknown Amish quiltmaker, American, Lancaster County, Pennsylvania, Circa 1890,
Pieced wools, 78 x 79 inches, 585.128

Lancaster Amish quilts are characteristically made from a very few pieces—large geometric fields of
solid-colored fabrics. None is as minimal as the Center Square, the purest of all their designs. The simple
box and surrounding borders are showplaces for their elegant, masterful quilting, which here covers
the surface of the quilt.

O

Name

Address

Telephone

Name

Address

Telephone

Name

Address

Telephone

Name

Address

Telephone

O

Name

Address

Telephone

Name

Address

Telephone

Name

Address

Telephone

Name

Address

Telephone

O

Name

Address

Telephone

Name

Address

Telephone

Name

Address

Telephone

Name

Address

Telephone

O

Name

Address

Telephone

Name

Address

Telephone

Name

Address

Telephone

Name

Address

Telephone

Bars (Variation)

Unknown Amish quiltmaker, American, Lancaster County, Pennsylvania, Circa 1910,
Pieced wools, 63 x 76 inches, 585.075

This is the only segmented example of a Bars we have seen. We have wondered if the squares that make up the bars could be swatches, fabric samples from which Lancaster Amish women ordered wools for their clothing and their quilts. In any case, here we get a good look at the colors and materials available to the Amish quiltmaker around the turn of the century.

Name

Address

Telephone

Name

Address

Telephone

Name

Address

Telephone

Name

Address

Telephone

P-Q

Name

Address

Telephone

Name

Address

Telephone

Name

Address

Telephone

Name

Address

Telephone

Name

Address

Telephone

Name

Address

Telephone

Name

Address

Telephone

Name

Address

Telephone

P-Q

Name

Address

Telephone

Name

Address

Telephone

Name

Address

Telephone

Name

Address

Telephone

S u n s h i n e   a n d   S h a d o w

Unknown Amish quiltmaker, American, Lancaster County, Pennsylvania, Circa 1910,
Pieced wools, 82 x 82 inches, 585.302

Among the conservative Lancaster Amish, an individual touch, such as the segmented inner border
here, represents a tolerated but significant break with convention. Aesthetics is a part of Amish life;
in Lancaster it is shaped by a commitment to excellence in workmanship and the highly held values of
fellowship and community. Conformity, in quiltmaking and throughout Amish life, ensures harmony.
There are very few absolutely unique Amish quilts.

Name

Address

Telephone

Name

Address

Telephone

Name

Address

Telephone

Name

Address

Telephone

R

Name

Address

Telephone

Name

Address

Telephone

Name

Address

Telephone

Name

Address

Telephone

R

Name

Address

Telephone

Name

Address

Telephone

Name

Address

Telephone

Name

Address

Telephone

R

Name

Address

Telephone

Name

Address

Telephone

Name

Address

Telephone

Name

Address

Telephone

R

Name

Address

Telephone

Name

Address

Telephone

Name

Address

Telephone

Name

Address

Telephone

R

Name

Address

Telephone

Name

Address

Telephone

Name

Address

Telephone

Name

Address

Telephone

D i a m o n d   i n   t h e   S q u a r e

Unknown Amish quiltmaker, American, Lancaster County, Pennsylvania, Circa 1940,
Pieced wools and rayons, 80 x 80 inches, 585.227

Later Lancaster quilts are often quilted in floral rather than geometric or abstract designs. They are also typically less densely quilted than their predecessors. One contributing factor may be that it is more difficult to make tiny, fine quilting stitches in the synthetic fabrics Amish women were using in the later period.

S

Name

Address

Telephone

Name

Address

Telephone

Name

Address

Telephone

Name

Address

Telephone

S

Name

Address

Telephone

Name

Address

Telephone

Name

Address

Telephone

Name

Address

Telephone

Name

Address

Telephone

Name

Address

Telephone

Name

Address

Telephone

Name

Address

Telephone

S

Name

Address

Telephone

Name

Address

Telephone

Name

Address

Telephone

Name

Address

Telephone

Name

Address

Telephone

Name

Address

Telephone

Name

Address

Telephone

Name

Address

Telephone

S

Name

Address

Telephone

Name

Address

Telephone

Name

Address

Telephone

Name

Address

Telephone

B a r s

Unknown Amish quiltmaker, American, Lancaster County, Pennsylvania, Circa 1940,
Pieced wools, 81 x 87 inches, 585.295

Printed or figured cloth is considered "worldly" by all Amish groups and is universally eschewed by them. Elaborate quilting, however—far beyond what is necessary to hold the three layers together—*is* permitted. Plain surfaces take on a quietly patterned look, with embossed geometric quilting motifs, as well as rather extravagant plumes and flowers.

T

Name

Address

Telephone

Name

Address

Telephone

Name

Address

Telephone

Name

Address

Telephone

T

Name

Address

Telephone

Name

Address

Telephone

Name

Address

Telephone

Name

Address

Telephone

T

Name

Address

Telephone

Name

Address

Telephone

Name

Address

Telephone

Name

Address

Telephone

T

Name

Address

Telephone

Name

Address

Telephone

Name

Address

Telephone

Name

Address

Telephone

Name

Address

Telephone

Name

Address

Telephone

Name

Address

Telephone

Name

Address

Telephone

T

Name

Address

Telephone

Name

Address

Telephone

Name

Address

Telephone

Name

Address

Telephone

C r a z y   Q u i l t

Unknown Amish quiltmaker, American, Lancaster County, Pennsylvania, Circa 1920,
Pieced wools, 70 x 80 inches, 585.279

In pottery, "crazed" glazes crackle into odd and unpredictable shapes. The term "crazy" in patchwork probably refers to the similarly random-shaped pieces that compose the quilt. In Lancaster, these bits and pieces tend to be organized into contained "crazy" squares relieved by the plain, unpieced blocks and half-blocks set next to them.

Name

Address

Telephone

Name

Address

Telephone

Name

Address

Telephone

Name

Address

Telephone

U-V

Name

Address

Telephone

Name

Address

Telephone

Name

Address

Telephone

Name

Address

Telephone

Name

Address

Telephone

Name

Address

Telephone

Name

Address

Telephone

Name

Address

Telephone

U-V

Name

Address

Telephone

Name

Address

Telephone

Name

Address

Telephone

Name

Address

Telephone

Sunshine and Shadow

Unknown Amish quiltmaker, American, Lancaster County, Pennsylvania, Circa 1930,
Pieced wools, 80 x 81 inches, 585.067

Most Amish Sunshine and Shadow quilts were made between 1920 and 1960 and are
a relatively late development in Lancaster design. Sunshine and Shadow can be seen as a complication
of the basic Diamond. Notice here how the Diamond form is heightened as the quiltmaker
"sandwiches" her colors in groups of three. Black is typically used as an accent, rather than
a predominant color, in Lancaster County Amish quilts.

Name

Address

Telephone

Name

Address

Telephone

Name

Address

Telephone

Name

Address

Telephone

W-X

Name

Address

Telephone

Name

Address

Telephone

Name

Address

Telephone

Name

Address

Telephone

Name

Address

Telephone

Name

Address

Telephone

Name

Address

Telephone

Name

Address

Telephone

W-X

Name

Address

Telephone

Name

Address

Telephone

Name

Address

Telephone

Name

Address

Telephone

Sawtooth Diamond

Made by Sarah Zook, Amish quiltmaker, American, Lancaster County, Pennsylvania,
Dated in quilting: "1925," Pieced wools, 82 x 82 inches, 585.214

Sawtooth was one of the variations on the basic Diamond in Lancaster County, though it is seen rather infrequently. This marvelously crafted example was very carefully planned to perfectly balance the Sawtooth edgings. The quilted "feathers" in the blue diamond also come to an elegant resolution. While it was customary for some Amish women in the Midwest to sign their quilts with initials, Lancaster women rarely did. The "SZ" quilted into this Lancaster piece, then, is an exception.

Name

Address

Telephone

Name

Address

Telephone

Name

Address

Telephone

Name

Address

Telephone

Y-Z

Name

Address

Telephone

Name

Address

Telephone

Name

Address

Telephone

Name

Address

Telephone

Name

Address

Telephone

Name

Address

Telephone

Name

Address

Telephone

Name

Address

Telephone

Y-Z

Name

Address

Telephone

Name

Address

Telephone

Name

Address

Telephone

Name

Address

Telephone

Name

Address

Telephone

Name

Address

Telephone

Name

Address

Telephone

Name

Address

Telephone